Clare Oliver

### *Machines on Mars*
Some of the most marvellous machines can go where
no human being has yet explored – into volcanoes,
the deep ocean floor and to Mars. Maybe machines
will be created to take us one day, but right now they
exist only in our imaginations.

## MACHINE QUIZ

**What job did the driver do before driving *Thrust*?**

a) airforce pilot
b) skateboard designer
c) rocket scientist

**Why do racing drivers spin their wheels at the starting line?**

a) to intimidate other drivers
b) engines perform best at high revolutions
c) to get rid of any rubber that might burn

**Why was the Paris-Madrid road race banned in 1903?**

a) France and Spain were at war
b) there was a worldwide petrol shortage
c) there'd been too many accidents in previous years

*(answers on page 32)*

## WINNING FORMULA

Formula One racing is the sporting showcase for speedsters *without* jet engines. Grand Prix cars are moulded out of carbon fibres to be amazingly light. Drivers are often twice as heavy as their car! At high speeds, a driver dare not let go of the steering wheel, so the gears are controlled by a switch on the wheel itself. An on-board computer monitors the car's suspension.

## EARLY DAYS

The first car race was in France, in 1895, over a 1,178-km route from Paris to Bordeaux and back. The average speed of the winning car was 24 km/h! Today's Grand Prix drivers roar along at 10 times that.

## GOING SUPERSONIC

Travelling faster than the speed of sound makes air rush over each part of the vehicle at different speeds. This creates bumpy shock waves that affect the car's lift and drag. When *Thrust SSC* went supersonic, the shock waves raised a 100-metre-high plume of desert dust. At such high speeds, there's a danger of taking off!

*Mika Hakkinen in his McLaren car*

# BRRRM! BRRRM!

Since the thrill of the first chariot race we've wanted ever-faster machines. Today's dragsters, hotrods, Formula One racing cars and supersonic rocket cars all zoom along at breathtaking speeds.

Thrust SSC

## LAND ROCKET

On 15 October 1997, British driver Andy Green set the first supersonic land speed record. He drove *Thrust SSC* at 1,227.985 km/h to complete the one-mile (1.6-km) course in the Black Rock Desert, Nevada. *Thrust* was built by Richard Noble, a previous land-speed champ. He salvaged two jet engines from a scrapped *Phantom* fighter plane.

### STICK YOUR NECK OUT

**Young racing drivers must exercise their neck muscles to withstand the sheer force of taking a corner at high-speed.**

# HIGH TYRES

Of all the machines on four wheels, monster trucks win the prize for whopping wheels! Four-wheel drive vehicles are COOL for off-road mayhem and fun!

## DODGY GIANT

Sheik Hamad Bin Hamdan Al Nahyan of the United Arab Emirates needs a tall ladder to get into his huge replica of a Dodge Power wagon. It's the biggest truck in the world and this monstrous machine really works!

*The largest truck in the world*

### OPERA-TION RALLY

**The longest truck rally ever – over 30,000 km – was in 1977. The race was from London's Royal Opera House to the Sydney Opera House in Australia. It took the winners six weeks to get there!**

## RIOTOUS RALLIES

A bumpy ride is all part of the fun of rallies held both on- and off-road. Often, the driver and navigator don't know the route until they get to the starting line! The first rally, held in 1907, was from Peking to Paris – about 12,000 km. Held since 1953, the longest regular rally is the 6,200-km East African Safari. But the key event for rally-drivers is the Monte Carlo Rally.

# MONSTER CRUNCH

Since the late 1970s, monster truck enthusiasts have been customising their pick-up trucks. An American car dealer, Bob Chandler, fitted extra-large tyres on his Ford F250 pick-up truck. To promote his business he drove it over a couple of scrap cars in a field. A few months later, he was car-crushing in his truck, *Bigfoot*, to a packed stadium.

# MACHINE QUIZ

**What safety features must a monster truck have?**

a) remote-control shutdown switch
b) in-cab shutdown switch
c) roll cage

**What safety items must a monster-truck driver wear?**

a) fireproof suit
b) goggles
c) helmet

**When was the first Monte Carlo Rally?**

a) 1901
b) 1907
c) 1911

*(answers on page 32)*

# NAME GAME

Today's monster trucks are often purpose–built and constructed of lightweight fibre-glass. Enthusiasts like to give their creations names – and let's face it, *Fairy Princess* just wouldn't sound right! These menacing-looking machines go into battle with names such as *Destroyer*, *Rampage*, *GroundPounder*, and *Goliath!*

# SCARY SAFARI

The biggest four-wheel-drive event in the USA is the Easter Jeep Safari in Moab, Utah. This is a whole week of events and races, but the scariest of them all is the Golden Spike trail. It features the Golden Crack, a one-metre-wide crevice, and the Double Whammy in which many 'jeepers' come unstuck!

*...lly racing in Tunisia*

5

*A US truck*

# MOBILE HOMES

Because they can be on the road for days, long-haul truckers need their lorry to be super-comfortable. The cab often has a sleeping bunk behind the driver's seat, and curtains. Instead of a passenger seat, some lorries have electric rings for heating up a meal. Others have a fridge, or even a sink with running water on board!

## MACHINE QUIZ

**What powered nineteenth-century fire engines?**

a) pedal-power
b) steam-propellers
c) horses

**What is a 'cooking seat'?**

a) a heated seat that keeps drivers warm
b) a cooker in the cab of a juggernaut
c) a juggernaut cab with no blinds

**What was the first juggernaut?**

a) Nero's chariot
b) an elephant
c) a chariot carrying the god Vishnu

*(answers on page 32)*

# DUMPER TRUCKS

Dumper trucks carry heavy loads such as rock and earth. Huge tyres cushion the weight. Their tread (the pattern cut into the rubber surface) is designed to force rainwater out from between the tyre and the road surface to make it less slippery.

*An Australian road-train*

# JUGGERNAUTS

The largest lorries, known as juggernauts, transport loads as heavy as two African elephants. The 10-tonne weight of one loaded juggernaut pressing down on the surface of the road causes the same amount of wear and tear on the tarmac as 64 million small cars!

# ON THE ROAD

It's no wonder little children like playing with toy trucks. Great big children (otherwise known as adults) love messing about in these chunky, powerful vehicles, too!

## WICKED WAGONS

In the Australian outback, goods are transported on giant road-trains. The truck at the front works like a train locomotive, and pulls lots of trailers behind it. At the front of the road-train are roo bars that protect the engine if the truck accidentally hits an animal. Kangaroos can be a big problem!

### TALL TYRE

A dumper truck's tyres may be over 3.6 metres high. That's about two-and-a-half times taller than you!

# MILITARY MIGHT

*British Army tank,* Challenger 1

Army engineering leads the way with
the most secret, stunning designs.
Of all off-road vehicles, tanks are toughest
and can manoeuvre over the trickiest of terrains.

## SEND IN THE HEAVIES

**British Army tank
*Challenger II* weighs
in at 62 tonnes. That's
heavier than a dozen
African elephants!**

## SUPER TROOPER

Armoured tanks were first used
in World War I. Muddy trench
warfare made it impossible to
use vehicles with ordinary wheels.
First, tractors were adapted for
the job. Later, purpose-built tanks
were used to cross the uneven
landscape. Early models could only
travel at about 6 km/h. Because
they are so heavy and bulky, tanks
will never be champion speedsters
but they do now zip along
at more than 70 km/h!

## TANKS ON TARGET

State-of-the-art infrared nightsights and laser
range finders help to ensure that when a tank
fires, it hits. Some weapons self-load, but most tanks
still need a gun loader in the crew.

# BIGGER GUNS

The 1918 *Renault* FT tank had a 37-mm gun; whereas some tanks today have guns three times as big. Some also have smart skins. In the 1980s, Israeli tanks were the first to use this reactive armour. Two layers of steel plating sandwich a layer of explosives, designed to explode outwards if the tank is hit.

## JEEPERS CREEPERS!

Jeeps were developed by the US Army for World War II. These tough and light four-wheel drive vehicles are ideal for reconnaissance missions and for transporting weapons or people across rough terrain. They can maintain a speed of 105 km/h on the road and can be armour-plated for combat missions. Some are even fitted with a waterproof hull and propeller, so they can be used in water as well as on land!

*A US Army tank*

## MACHINE QUIZ

**What is a tankbuster?**

a) a fighter plane that blows up tanks

b) a radar operator who spies on enemy tanks

c) a machine that breaks up tanks for recycling

**Why is a jeep called a jeep?**

a) because it's a GP (general purpose) vehicle

b) it was designed by Karl Jeepz

c) it was short for 'Jesus weeps'

**What does SAM stand for?**

a) Sergeants Active on Manoeuvres

b) Surface-to-Air Missile

c) Supersonic Aircraft Missile

*(answers on page 32)*

# MACHINE QUIZ

**Who paved the way for radar by proving radio waves exist?**

a) Ricardo Radio
b) Stanley Stereo
c) Heinrich Hertz

**What non-military use does radar have?**

a) high-tech canes for visually-impaired people
b) to catch speeding cars
c) tracking serious storms

**How much does a stealth plane cost?**

a) $20m to $45m
b) $45m to $2bn
c) $2bn to $8bn

*(answers on page 32)*

# HOW RADAR WORKS

Radar systems were developed in the 1920s after the Italian engineer Guglielmo Marconi realised that radio waves could be used to detect objects. A radar transmitter sends out waves of electromagnetic energy at regular intervals. As the waves hit objects in their path, echoes bounce back towards the transmitter and are picked up by its super-sensitive receiver. These days, high-speed computers work out the position of planes and ships according to the time it takes for the echo to return.

# B2 BOMBERS

Pride of the US Air Force is its fleet of 21 Lockheed *B2* bombers, the stealthiest planes in the skies. Flat-shaped, with no right angles, their exterior is coated with special paint and graphite (like the 'lead' in your pencil) to scatter and distort radar signals. A pair of *B2*s can do as much bomb damage as a fleet of 55 planes.

*Artist's impression of the* Aurora *spy plane*

# 21ST-CENTURY SKY SPY

The world's most advanced military spy plane is the *Aurora*. Capable of speeds of up to 8,500 km/h, it needs a 12-km runway for take off and flies at an altitude of 40,000 metres. Still being developed by the US military, its exact design remains top secret.

# BUILT FOR STEALTH

Stealth warships and planes achieve what once seemed impossible. They are almost undetectable by enemy radar!

Sea Shadow

## A SHIP YOU CAN'T SEE!

A stealth ship can be seen by eye but not by radar. So, stealth vehicles travel under cover of darkness or fog. They can outfox radar because of their angular shape and slippery surface. The US Navy's *Sea Shadow* is designed like a catamaran. With two long narrow hulls instead of a single wide one, less of the vessel comes into contact with the water, which helps it to glide easily over the waves.

**OOPS!**

**State-of-the-art *B2* stealth bombers have a fatal flaw. If left out in the rain too long, their radar-deflecting paint washes off!**

# SEA MONSTERS

Forget about scary underwater predators of the animal
kingdom, the deadliest monsters of the deep - and the
surface, too - are all man-made.

## PLANE SAILING

Because big submarines and aircraft carriers are nuclear-powered they
can stay out at sea for ages without needing to dock and refuel. Carriers
are huge floating airports that can carry as many as 100 fighter planes at
a time. The armoured deck is a giant runway from which the planes are
catapulted into the air. When the planes return, a hook is lowered which
catches onto a strong wire on the deck. This stops the planes zooming
off the edge! To one side of the flight deck is the 'island', the control tower
from where planes are guided in and out. The biggest aircraft carriers,
such as the US Navy's *Nimitz* Class carriers, need a crew of 6,000!

**VIKING LONGBOAT**
Supertanker *Jahre Viking* is
so enormous, it's in a field
of its own. In fact, from
bow to stern, it's as long as
four football pitches!

## PORTS AND PIPES

A fully-laden supertanker sits far too deep in the water to enter a
harbour. Its submerged hull can be more than 22 metres below the
surface. The huge oil tankers have to pump their liquid
loads along many kilometres of underwater
pipeline directly into tanks
on land.

*HMS* Torbay, *nuclear submarine*

*A supertanker at dock*

# OIL BE BACK

The most enormous ships at sea are supertankers. The biggest of them all is *Jahre Viking* which weighs 565,000 tonnes – that's more than 1,000 jumbo jets! These tankers are designed to carry super-heavy liquid loads. Some transport crude oil to refineries; and some carry natural gas that has been cooled to a liquid.

# SINKING FEELING

Unlike most sea-going vessels, submarines are designed to sink! When a sub needs to dive, a computer-controlled ballast tank floods with water. Since water is heavier than air, the sub sinks. When the sub needs to rise to the surface, high-pressure air hoses blast the water out of the tanks. The biggest, fastest underwater craft are nuclear-powered. Introduced in the 1980s, Russian *Typhoon* Class subs are serious missile machines, carrying terrifying ballistic missiles. They cruise the oceans at about 74 km/h and are a whopping 170 metres long.

# MACHINE QUIZ

**Why don't submarine crews run out of air?**

a) they wear oxygen tanks
b) a machine extracts oxygen from seawater
c) only people with extra-strong lungs are recruited

**What was the first submarine called?**

a) the *Turtle*
b) the *Stingray*
c) *Moby Dick*

**In 1910, who flew the first plane to take off from a ship?**

a) Wilbur Wright
b) Eugene Ely
c) Billie-Jean Fly

*(answers on page 32)*

*Off-shore powerboat racing*

# FORMULA ONE ON WATER

Each year there are 10 Grand Prix powerboat races. Top of the Class One powerboats – the watery equivalent of Formula One – is *Spirit of Norway*. Like most powerboats, it has twin hulls made of lightweight carbon fibre. The catamaran design minimises drag, and the craft takes just 14 seconds to accelerate up to 100 km/h. Formula One cars can do that in less than three seconds.

# MACHINE QUIZ

**What does the Tamil word *kattumaran*, from which we took 'catamaran', mean?**

a) trees tied together
b) raised above the waves
c) stretched catskin hull

**In what year was the first off-shore powerboat race?**

a) 1904
b) 1914
c) 1924

**What is the role of the throttleman in powerboat racing?**

a) to steer
b) to control the boat's gears
c) to shout out the boat's position

*(answers on page 32)*

## LOST LIVES

The exhilarating sport of powerboat racing has claimed many lives. In 1964, Donald Campbell, a record-breaking racer on both land and water, broke the land-speed record in his *Bluebird-Proteus CN7*, travelling at nearly 650 km/h. Three years later, he died in his jetboat *Bluebird* after reaching more than 480 km/h.

## UNBEATABLE?

The 1978 water-speed record set by Ken Warby in *Spirit of Australia* is yet to be broken. Now in his fifties, Warby is building a new boat he hopes will beat it. In 1980, Lee Taylor tried in *Discovery II*, designed to reach 1,000 km/h. At 434 km/h, the boat hit a swell, disintegrated and sank, taking Taylor with it. Craig Arfons tried in *Rain-X Record Challenger*. Its safety parachute failed and Arfons was killed when the boat exploded.

# CREST OF A WAVE

As jet skis and powerboats zip effortlessly across the surf at extraordinary speeds, it's easy to see why they are the playthings of the rich and powerful!

Jet-skiing

## NO-SNOW SKIS

Jet skis are wicked! Wickedly fast and dangerous. Jet-skiing is like riding a motorbike – on water! Many motorcycle manufacturers, such as Kawasaki, use their technical know-how to make jet skis. The world record for the fastest jet-skier is 106.36 km/h, but even that could be beaten by the fastest fish in the sea – the sailfish. The machines work by sucking in a jet of water which then passes over a turbine to drive the motor.

## HIGH-POWERED HYDROFOIL

**The world water-speed record is held by *Spirit of Australia*. At full pelt, about 514 km/h, it could travel the length of the Nile in just 13 hours.**

# ON YER BIKE!

You never forget how to ride a bike but riding a superfast motorbike is so thrilling you could forget your own name! For motorbike enthusiasts, two wheels are definitely better than four, whether they're racing on road, track, or cross-country.

## SPEED LEADS

Speedway is a sport for small, light motorbikes, often with no brakes! The bikes race round on a flat, oval, dirt track about 320 metres long. The first speedway event was held in Australia in the 1920s. Since then it has become a top spectator sport. In the United Kingdom, only

## ICE SPIKES

One of the weirdest forms of motorcycle racing began in Scandinavia in the 1930s. Ice-racing bikes have spiked tyres and race each other round frozen lakes or on iced stadium tracks!

A road-racing Honda

## BIKE TYPES

There are four different classes of motorcycle. Trail bikes are the lightest and have the smallest engines. Next are road bikes, then touring bikes. Finally, come the champion speedsters – racing bikes. Top racing bikes, or superbikes, have engines of up to 160 horsepower. That's powerful!

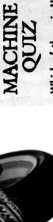

# HARLEYS & HOGS

For motorbike enthusiasts, Harley-Davidson bikes are supreme. These American bikes have been in production for nearly a century! Childhood friends, William Harley and Arthur Davidson used to spend their spare time building a motorised bike. The Harley-Davidson Company produced its first bike in 1903. Ten years later the bike had travelled 100,000 miles and not a single part needed fixing! Today, the worldwide club for enthusiasts, HOG (Harley Owners Group), has over 300,000 members.

*Harley-Davidson*

**BRILLIANT BIKES**

The fastest motorbikes can travel at about 300 km/h. That's as fast as the high-speed *Eurostar* trains!

## MACHINE QUIZ

**Which of these is NOT a Harley-Davidson?**

a) *Electra Glide Classic*
b) *Fat Boy*
c) *Road Emperor*

**What happened to the first petrol-engined motorbike in 1903?**

a) police confiscated it because the owner was speeding at 15 km/h
b) it burnt in a fire because it had a wooden frame
c) it became the first vehicle ever to be knighted

**What was the first Dunlop tyre made of?**

a) melted wellingtons
b) elastic bands
c) garden hose

*(answers on page 32)*

# CHOOO! CHOOO!

Railways have come a long way since 1825 when the first passenger locomotive, Stephenson's *Active*, made its maiden journey from Darlington to Stockton - at a wild 24 km/h!

## MACHINE QUIZ

**What was the top speed achieved by the steam train, *Mallard*?**

a) 200 km/h
b) 150 km/h
c) 50 km/h

**What is a pantograph?**

a) the overhead power supply cable for electric trains
b) a comparison of regulation underwear for railworkers
c) a measure of how much steam an engine needs

**What do 'pushers' do at Japanese stations?**

a) push passengers into the crowded trains
b) push the train when it won't start
c) push luggage trolleys

*(answers on page 32)*

## MOVERS & SHAKERS

Some of today's trains swish along at astonishing speeds. With new smooth tracks and air-cushion suspension, speed and comfort have replaced the wobbly fun of lurching along in old trains. On regular routes, high-speed trains reach around 300 km/h – the norm for *Nozomi* Class *Shinkansens* (bullet trains) in Japan; for the French TGV *Atlantique* and *Nord* trains; and for *Eurostar* in France.

The MLU-002

## RUSSIAN ROUTE

The longest regular train journey is Moscow to Vladivostock. The *Trans-Siberian Express* takes almost a week to travel more than 9,400 km.

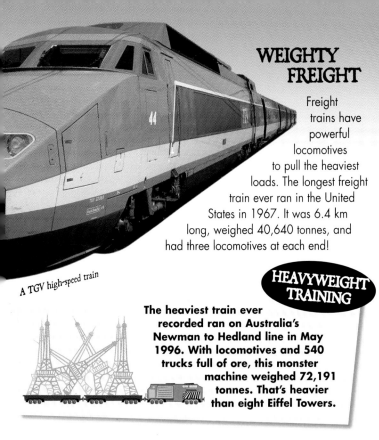

## WEIGHTY FREIGHT

Freight trains have powerful locomotives to pull the heaviest loads. The longest freight train ever ran in the United States in 1967. It was 6.4 km long, weighed 40,640 tonnes, and had three locomotives at each end!

A TGV high-speed train

### HEAVYWEIGHT TRAINING

**The heaviest train ever recorded ran on Australia's Newman to Hedland line in May 1996. With locomotives and 540 trucks full of ore, this monster machine weighed 72,191 tonnes. That's heavier than eight Eiffel Towers.**

## FLOATING ON AIR

Maglevs (magnetic levitation trains) don't need engines. Electromagnets in the track attract the train forwards, while magnets behind push it. With no vibration or friction to slow them down, trains such as Japan's maglev, *MLU-002*, have reached speeds of 550 km/h in test runs! When the service is finally launched, it will halve the journey time from Osaka to Tokyo. But it looks as though Germany will be first to have a maglev passenger service. The *Transrapid* will link Berlin and Hamburg by the year 2005, with trains completing the 300-km journey in an hour.

# MECHANICAL WORKHORSE

Some mighty machines don't set glorious records nor look fabulously streamlined. Functional machines, such as cranes, diggers and giant drills, are great but it's the buildings and tunnels they help to construct that get the attention!

## WHEELS & WHALES

**The crane used to support the London Eye ferris wheel is superstrong. It can lift weights of nearly 1,000 tonnes. That's the same as seven blue whales!**

## HOW BORING!

A tunnel-boring machine (TBM) is a giant drill used to bore through earth and rock to make an underground cavity. Nicknamed 'the mole', the TBM used to dig out the Eurotunnel had more than 100 cutting rollers and 200 teeth on its cutting head.

The 'mole'

## LASER LINE-UP

When boring out the Channel Tunnel, French and English engineers had to ensure they would meet in the middle. Lasers kept the 1,300-tonne machines exactly on course and hydraulic jacks moved them forward. When even the most powerful machines can't bore through truly hard rock, such as granite, engineers have to use explosives – carefully!

# ACE INVENTIONS

Cranes work using a system of levers and pulleys. These ingenious inventions are key to how machines work to make lifting heavy weights possible. Levers are simply brilliant. Expert archaeologists reckon Stone Age people used tree branches as levers to move heavy rocks, and pulleys were used to build the Acropolis in ancient Greece. A heavy weight that would otherwise stay firmly on the ground can be lifted with a rope and pulley. A rope is attached, then threaded round the grooved rim of a pulley wheel fixed above it. Pulling down on the other end of the rope will raise the weight as the rope running over the wheel does most of the work.

## EYE, EYE

Today's cranes are motorised. Earlier cranes used steam power. And before that, medieval people walked endlessly on treadmills to power them! Cranes have to lift some very heavy objects – such as the London Eye ferris wheel. Built to mark the millennium, this capital landmark by the Thames River took almost a week to lift. The heavyweight crane that took the strain was state-of-the-art *Taklift 1*.

# MACHINE QUIZ

**How do operators of tall cranes pee?**

a) they just have to wait
b) they take a potty up with them
c) they climb down to the loo

**What is the main arm of a crane called?**

a) jib
b) plank
c) girder-grabber

**What do piledriving machines do?**

a) hammer a building's foundation posts into the ground
b) carry heaps of earth away from digging machines
c) dispose of rubbish from building sites

(answers on page 32)

Taklift 1 *ready for lift off!*

21

# JET-SET

Jet engines suck in air at the front of the plane and into the combustion chamber where the fuel is burned. Hot exhaust gases shoot out of the back, jetting the plane forwards. German engineer Ernst Heinkel built the first jet-engined aircraft – the *HE178*, used during World War II. The first jet passenger airliners – the De Havilland *Comet* and the Boeing *707* – took to the air over 50 years ago. Thanks to the invention of the jet engine holidaymakers can see the world.

## MACHINE QUIZ

**Supersonic means as fast as the speed of sound. How fast is hypersonic?**

a) the same
b) the same, but in space, not in Earth's atmosphere
c) five times the speed of sound

**How many people does it take to build an *Airbus 340*?**

a) 300
b) 3,000
c) 30,000

**Who was the first aviator to fly non-stop across the Channel and back?**

a) Charles Stewart Rolls
b) Sir Henry Royce
c) Louis Blériot

(answers on page 32)

*The Bell Boeing 609*

## FULL TILT

The Bell Boeing *609* is a brand-new breed of flying machine called a tiltrotor. It's half-plane, half-helicopter. At take-off, it behaves like a helicopter. Its rotor blades allow it to take off vertically, so there's no need for a runway. Once the *609* is in flight, the rotors tilt down to create propeller-driven wings – neat!

# IS IT A BIRD?

Soaring through the air like a bird... Until the Wright brothers made aviation history in 1903 in a flimsy wooden biplane, powered flight seemed like a dream.

Concorde

## GOING SUPERSONIC!

The first aircraft to break the sound barrier was military – the Bell *XS-1* plane, way back in 1947. *Concorde* was the first supersonic passenger plane. It made its maiden flight in 1969 but did not go into regular service until seven years later. Its maximum speed is 2,179 km/h.

### THE WRIGHT DISTANCE

**The distance between the wingtips of a Boeing *747* is further than Orville and Wilbur Wright's first flight!**

## HOT AIR?

Still at top-secret design stage, the *Airbus A3XX* promises plenty of luxury. Planned for launch in 2004, this 21st-century aircraft will seat over 650 pampered passengers and provide them with an on-board gym, nursery and medical centre. In-flight meals on trays may become a thing of the past, too, as a fast-food restaurant and shop are planned!

# TRAVEL SICKNESS

Accelerating to supersonic speeds does weird things to human bodies! People photographed in military planes going faster than the speed of sound (Mach 1) do not look pretty! The two-seater Lockheed *SR-71 Blackbird* streaks across the sky at Mach 3 (three times the speed of sound). Its pilots say once the plane is cruising it feels as if they're not moving at all. But reaching Mach 3 plays havoc with facial features, and many first-timers even throw up in the cockpit!

## PAINT IT BLACK

The Lockheed *SR-71* is nicknamed *Blackbird* because it's painted black. The paint stops the plane overheating by allowing heat to escape into the atmosphere.

# FAST FLIERS

Fancy flying off on holiday via space? For faster flights, engineers reckon the only way is UP! So the passenger planes of the future will be rocket-powered.

## SKIMMING THE POND

American scientist Preston Carter is building one of the next generation of fast planes, the hypersonic jet. It's not expected to be in operation before 2025. His *HyperSoar* will take off from a normal runway and quickly speed up to Mach 10 (about 11,600 km/h). This will use lots of rocket fuel but the plane saves power by skimming along above Earth's atmosphere. *HyperSoar's* engines will cut out at 35,000 metres and pure momentum will carry it on further and higher. When it glides back down to 35,000 metres, its rockets will fire up again.

*Breaking the sound barrier*

## MACHINE QUIZ

**Name the first Soviet supersonic jet fighter.**

a) the *Mig-19*
b) the *Mig-21*
c) the *Mig-29*

**The first supersonic plane, Bell *X-1*, was built to look like ...?**

a) a flying goose
b) a bullet with wings
c) a kite

**Which pilot first flew at Mach 1?**

a) Amy Johnson
b) Chuck Yeager
c) Donald Campbell

*(answers on page 32)*

## HOTTING UP

At high altitudes, the temperature outside a supersonic plane can be as low as –55 °C, but the friction of flying so fast toasts the exterior of the plane to a searing 425 °C. The *Blackbird* is built from painted titanium, a highly heat-resistant metal. This solves the problem of extreme temperatures for the pilot. To counteract the low air pressure inside the craft, he or she wears a protective pressure suit.

# MACHINE QUIZ

**What was the first dog in space called?**

a) Striker
b) Laika
c) Yuri

**How many flights will a shuttle make in its lifetime?**

a) 50
b) 150
c) 200

**What was the only Soviet space shuttle that flew called?**

a) *Mir*
b) *Sputnik*
c) *Buran*

*(answers on page 32)*

*Titan IV rocket launch*

# INTO SPACE...& BACK

NASA's Space Shuttle was the first reusable spacecraft. *Columbia* blasted into space in 1981, weighing 2,000 tonnes. Lifting so much weight off the ground needs as much thrust as for 140 jumbo jets! Two booster rockets do all the hard work, then fall away after about two minutes. A fleet of four shuttles is in use today: *Columbia*, *Discovery*, *Atlantis* and *Endeavour*. When a mission is complete, the shuttles glide back down to Earth and land on a runway.

# THE FUTURE?

NASA are now testing machines to take over when shuttles retire. Unlike the Space Shuttle, the *X-33* will not drop its boosters or fuel tanks. Planning a shuttle flight takes three months and thousands of people, but the *X-33* will only need a staff of 50 and could be prepared for a mission in two days. So, the *X-33* may well be used to transport space tourists – at a speed of Mach 15!

# ROCKET POWER

Thousands of rockets have been launched into space since the 1950s. In 1969, the *Saturn V* rocket lifted off from Kennedy Space Center, Florida, carrying the precious *Apollo 11* for its historic journey to the Moon. Today, most rockets transport satellites into space. *Ariane 5* can launch four satellites at once.

# LIFT OFF!

Space is the ultimate challenge. In 1957 the Russians led the way by launching the first-ever satellite, *Sputnik 1* into orbit. The space race had begun!

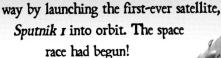

*The X-38 carried by a B-52 bomber*

## ESCAPE

If astronauts ever need to escape from space in an emergency, the *X-38* will be their space lifeboat! The wingless craft has already been tested by being dropped from a *B-52* bomber! Parachutes opened at an altitude of about 4,500 metres, allowing the *X-38* to gently glide down to Earth. When the real thing is operational, a rocket engine will transport the craft and its passengers from, say, a space station, to the Earth's atmosphere where the parachutes will take over.

**CRISPY WINGS**

The early rocket plane the *X-15* had a design flaw. Its wings burnt off as it re-entered Earth's atmosphere!

# REAL-LIFE ROBOTS

Some places are just too dangerous to work in - deep below the ocean, at the frozen poles, in bubbling volcanoes, or in space. So, roll on the highest-tech machines of all - robots.

## ROBOTS IN SPACE

Robots can go where no one has gone before! They can withstand lack of oxygen or extremes of temperature. On 4 July 1997 the robot rover *Sojourner* landed on Mars. The six-wheeled machine's mission was to send back pictures of the Red Planet. NASA scientists 380,000 km away down on Earth, directed the robot by remote-control.

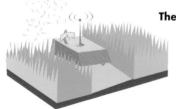

The *Robomow* is the ideal gift for a busy parent - if you have a spare £1,000! This handy little robot mows the lawn all by itself!

**LIVE FOR THE MOW-MENT**

## BUSY BUILDERS

Already over half a million robots are at work here on Earth. The most popular is the *Puma*, whose name stands for Programmable Universal Machine for Assembly. Designed in the 1970s, it is used in labs and on factory assembly lines. Over 50 per cent of the world's robots work in Japan.

# RADIOACTIVE ROBOTS

During the deadly 1986 disaster at the Chernobyl nuclear power station in Ukraine, a huge fireball blew up the reactor.

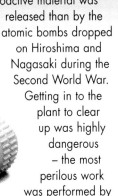

Sojourner

More radioactive material was released than by the atomic bombs dropped on Hiroshima and Nagasaki during the Second World War. Getting in to the plant to clear up was highly dangerous – the most perilous work was performed by robots *Houdini* and *Pioneer*.

## MACHINE QUIZ

**Which robot visits volcanoes?**

a) *Dante*
b) *Inferno*
c) *Vulcan*

**Which robot explores the sea bed?**

a) *Neoprene*
b) *Snoopy*
c) *Nero*

**Which robot will collect comet dust?**

a) *Stardust*
b) *Comet-Catcher*
c) *Trail-Chaser*

(answers on page 32)

## SUPER SLAVES

It would be great if robots could do all our boring jobs. *Tinker* was built in the 1970s to wash the car. Unfortunately, it took four hours to do it! The most advanced robotic home-help on the market is the *Electrolux*. It can't climb stairs, but will clean a whole floor of the house as long as all doors are open. But these complex machines are very expensive. Your 21st-century home may never boast a robot, but you could fit it out with smart appliances, such as intelligent cookers and self-cleaning carpets.

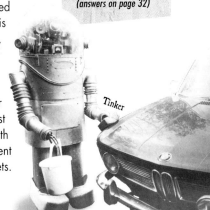

Tinker

# CYBORGS

What about robots of the future? Will it be possible to merge man and machine? Or will humanoid robots remain a sci-fi dream?

## MACHINE QUIZ

**What does AI stand for?**
a) Artificial Intelligence
b) Advanced Invention
c) Automated Individual

**What do you call a scientist who investigates cyborgs?**
a) a cybologist
b) a trekkie
c) a cyberneticist

**When was the word 'robot' coined?**
a) 1590
b) 1920
c) 1950

*(answers on page 32)*

## CYBORGS ON-SCREEN

Human-like robots have always been favourites in science-fiction films. Machines can be given special powers that make them more-than-human. For example *Seven*, the glam cyborg in *Star Trek: The Next Generation*, had circuits around her left eye to give her super-powerful vision. And the *Terminator* films predicted a future where cybercops and cyberbaddies battled it out.

## CYBORGS TODAY

If cyborgs are a mixture of a person and a machine, then they're already here! Modern medicine allows doctors to replace our faulty parts with new, electronic ones, such as pacemakers to regulate the heart. More advanced features, such as artificial lungs, or bionic eyes with in-built nightvision, are just around the corner. The big cyborg challenge is to build an artificial brain.

*Human nerve cell on a silicon chip*

# BRAIN STRAIN

Bio-engineering (growing human tissue in the lab) is the next stage. Already, those boffins in white coats have succeeded in growing human nerve cells on a silicon chip! But the human brain contains as many cells as there are stars in the Milky Way, so building one may be a bit of a problem. Another possibility would be to assemble cyborgs atom by atom but, again, the technology required is a long way off.

# TRICKY QUESTIONS

Before we create fully functioning cyborgs, there are interesting questions to ask. Could a cyborg have feelings? Would you call a cyborg 'it', 'he' or 'she'? Should a cyborg have rights? What would happen if there were lots of intelligent robots on Earth? What if the cyborgs evolved to become smarter than we are? Perhaps humans would become extinct and our cyborg creations would rule the world!

*Seven in Star Trek*

## ROBODOG

Humans aren't the only animals to inspire robo-scientists. There are already robo pets on the market, including Sony's tail-wagging robot dog, AIBO. At the moment it can only play, but Sony hope to develop language-learning software so that future robot dogs can learn to talk to their owners.

# QUIZ ANSWERS:

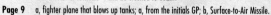

**Page 2**   a, airforce pilot; b, engines perform best at high revolutions; c, there'd been too many accidents in previous years.

**Page 5**   a, b, c, trick question – all three safety features are needed; a, b, c, trick question – the driver must wear all three items; c, 1911.

**Page 6**   a, b, c, trick question – fire engines were powered by all three methods; b, a cooker; c, Vishnu's chariot – *Jagannatha* is Sanskrit for the god Vishnu. Worshippers used to throw themselves in front of a chariot at festivals – and be crushed to death!

**Page 9**   a, fighter plane that blows up tanks; a, from the initials GP; b, Surface-to-Air Missile.

**Page 10**   c, Heinrich Hertz; a, b, c, trick question – radar is used for all three; c, S2–8 billion.

**Page 13**   b, a machine extracts oxygen from seawater; a, the *Turtle*; b, Eugene Ely.

**Page 14**   a, trees tied together; a, 1904; b, to control the boat's gears.

**Page 17**   c, *Road Emperor*; b, it burnt in a fire; c, garden hose.

**Page 18**   a, 200 km/h; a, overhead power supply cable; a, push passengers into the crowded trains.

**Page 21**   b, take a potty up with them; a, jib; a, hammer foundation posts into the ground.

**Page 22**   c, five times speed of sound; c, 30,000; a, Charles Stewart Rolls.

**Page 25**   a, the *Mig-19*; b, a bullet with wings; b, Chuck Yeager.

**Page 26**   b, Laika; c, 200; c, *Buran*.

**Page 29**   a, *Dante*; b, *Snoopy*; a, *Stardust*.

**Page 30**   a, Artificial Intelligence; c, cyberneticist; b, 1920.

## Acknowledgements

We would like to thank Phil Clucus, Helen Wire and Elizabeth Wiggans for their assistance. Cartoons by John Alston.

Copyright © 2000 ticktock *Publishing Ltd.*
First published in Great Britain by ticktock Publishing Ltd.,
The Offices in the Square, Hadlow, Tonbridge, Kent TN11 0DD, Great Britain.
All rights reserved.
No part of this publication may be reproduced, stored in a retrieval system, or transmitted in any form or by any means electronic, mechanical, photocopying, recording or otherwise, without prior written permission of the copyright owner.
A CIP catalogue record for this book is available from the British Library.
ISBN 1 86007 176 7

Picture Credits: t = top, b = bottom, c = centre, l = left, r= right, OFC = outside front cover, OBC = outside back cover, IFC = inside front cover

Allsport; 2/3t, 14tl, 16/17c. Defence Picture Library; 8/9t. Hulton Getty; 29br. MSI; 21br. Pictor; 6/7c & OFC, 6tl, 12/13b, 14/15c, 18/19t. Rex; 2/3b, 4/5t, 4/5b, 10/11c, 17b, 20/21c, 22cr, 22/23t, 30/31c. Science Photo Library; IFC, 10bl, 12/13t, 18/19b, 24t, 25bl, 26bl, 27t, 28/29c, 31t. Sipa Press; 8/9b.

Picture research by Image Select. Printed in Hong Kong.